# You Promised

*Phyllis Sunday*

Copyright © 2016 Phyllis Sunday
All rights reserved.

ISBN 13: 978-0692612415
ISBN 10: 0692612416

Illustrated by
Md. Hemayet Uddin

Interior Design by
Woven Red Author Services

*In memory of my aunt
Susanah Ekpeye*

Phyllis Sunday has spent over a decade working with children of all age groups.

Books by the author are:
*Book of Poems*
*The Snow*
*The Infant*
*Thank You, Lord*
*The Beggar*

You promised to give me

the moon and the stars.

You promised to sail the world with me, across the oceans and continents.

You promised to be there to love and treasure me

because I am yours forever.

You promised to hold my hand in the storm, shelter me from the winds, and never to let go.

You promised to give me

the world on a silver platter.

But when the
storms came
and the winds blew,
you let go
of my hand
and vanished
in the fog.

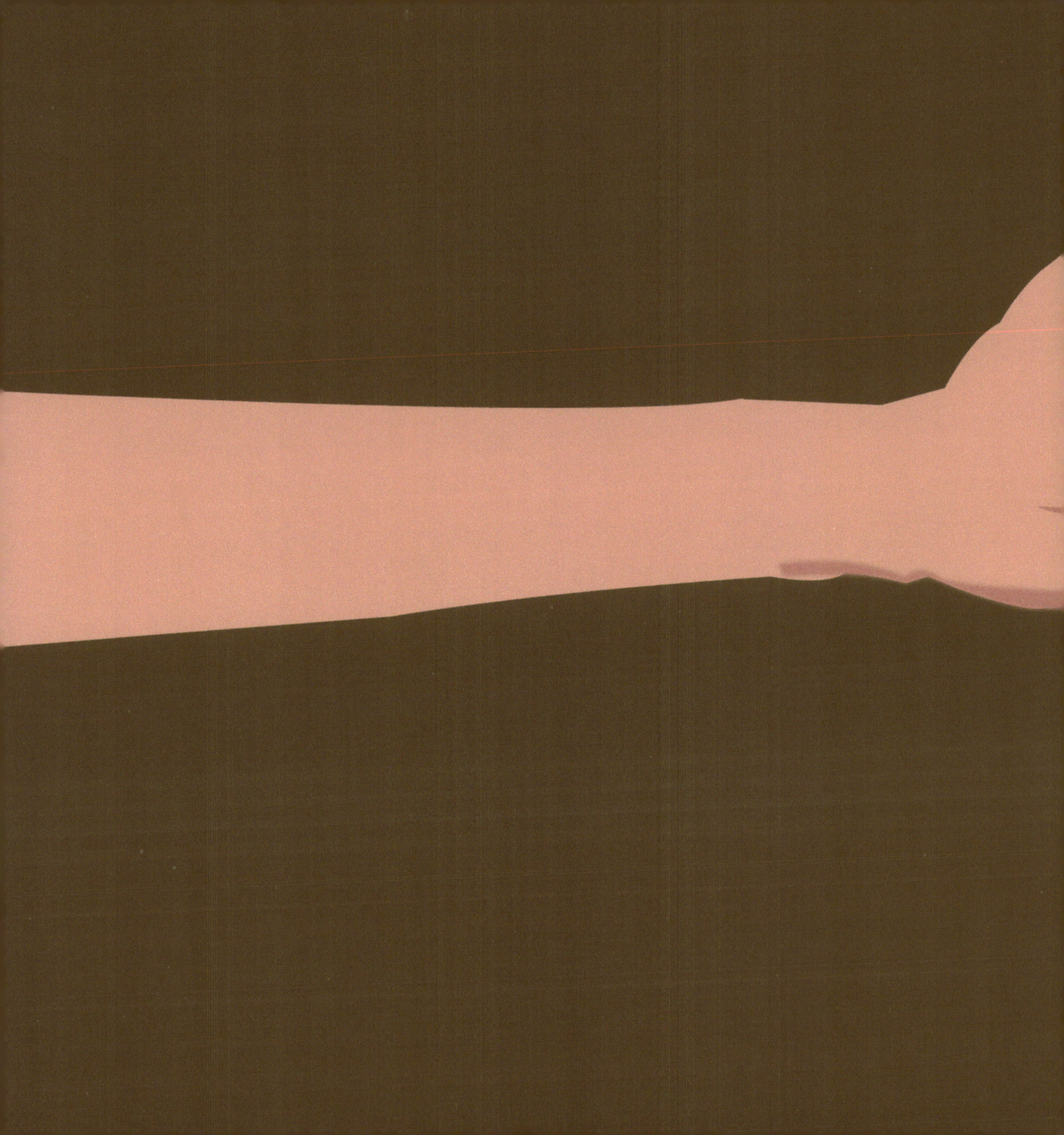

But you promised never to let go.

www.ingramcontent.com/pod-product-compliance
Lightning Source LLC
Chambersburg PA
CBHW041542040426
42446CB00002B/203